Prepare to Impress

Prepare to Impress

—job hunting for the ambitious, frustrated, unemployed and those facing redundancy

Rob and Tammy Ball, with Natalie Ball

AuthorHouse™
1663 Liberty Drive
Bloomington, IN 47403
www.authorhouse.com
Phone: 1-800-839-8640

Manuscript Prepared by Naturally Concerned Publishing

Naturally Concerned (for Alison) Ltd
12 Stacey Grange Gardens
Rednal
Birmingham
B45 9PN
UK

www.naturallyconcerned.com

First published by AuthorHouse   11/23/2011

ISBN: 978-1-4670-2009-1 (sc)
ISBN: 978-1-4670-2010-7 (ebk)

Printed in the United States of America

This book is printed on acid-free paper.

A CIP Catalogue of this book is available from the British Library

Dedications;

My inspirational women

RMB

My Love

TFB

For Mum

NELB

Contents

Introduction

There can have been few times as difficult for people to find employment as now. More redundancies, less business growth, overseas markets absorbing traditional work and the accelerating need for new skills are all combining to spread concern amongst those without a job or feel the threat of imminent unemployment. There are no jobs-for-life. So, given the levels of joblessness, it is highly competitive for each and every vacancy.

It wouldn't be a surprise if every unemployed person was feeling real despair and frustration. There are no easy solutions but this short book seeks to help those prepared to work at finding work. All anyone can do is apply themselves intelligently to the task and to do it to the best of their ability.

We will discuss the processes which are used by organisations to release staff. It may be, at least in part, the answer is avoiding dismissal and, therefore, the need to seek new employment.

We will look at the immediate impact and priorities when termination of employment occurs. As very few people will find a new position immediately we will deal with the on-going problems which may manifest themselves and, ultimately, what to do when a job offer is received.

It is most important to remember that whatever the state of the economy there are vacancies. The trick is to know where to find them and then to impress the potential employer.

Almost inevitably, there will be occasions when you are unable to secure a job for which you have applied. This will be difficult to deal with emotionally. However, recognising it is a normal part of the situation and it is the same for nearly everyone, will allow you to think through the implications and continue positively.

There are two key messages to remember;

1   Your job is finding a job

2   Proper Preparation Prevents Poor Performance
     (PPPPP)

This may be a bumpy road for you to travel. There are many people travelling in the same direction and not everyone will reach a desired destination. Some clear thinking can improve the chances of success immeasurably.

Application and behaviour do not guarantee success but do affect the likelihood of finding work, in any economic circumstances. A lack of focus will guarantee job hunting is a fruitless pursuit. Little things matter and will make the difference.

Chapter 1

Losing employment (or perhaps not)

There are no jobs-for-life

Losing your employment

In broad terms there are four ways an individual becomes unemployed;

Resignation

Contract termination

Dismissal for disciplinary or performance reasons

Redundancy

Resignation

People resign for many reasons, such as;

- Boredom
- Poor working relationships
- A desire for change
- An alternative job
- To return to education
- Personal circumstances
- Coercion. This may give rise to a claim for constructive dismissal, unfair dismissal or discrimination. Our advice is, don't give up a basically decent job too readily unless the situation is untenable and only then if you have tried to resolve the issues first. If the resignation has been forced on you, take professional advice. It is important to keep a note of instances of bad management behaviour such as inappropriate relationships, being given all of the horrid tasks, unreasonable targets and bullying.

Contract termination

If there is a defined period for a contract it allows the people involved to plan for its end.

Note this is not the same as a probationary period. Termination within a probationary period would come under dismissal for disciplinary or performance reasons.

There may also be complicating issues if a contract has a determined length but is consistently renewed or there is a promise of a permanent job. There are employers who might, in all innocence, misuse this type of arrangement.

Unless a waiver has been signed, a contract which extends beyond two years, and against which the individual works for more than two years, will acquire redundancy rights.

Dismissal for disciplinary or performance reasons

Employers cannot dismiss anyone legitimately without using a proper process. Such a process needs to be fair and transparent, and must be carried out in an objective and equitable manner. We have left the days when an unenlightened manager could just call someone in and sack them.

The most often discussed type of dismissals are for gross misconduct and poor performance. If an individual is faced with action of this nature it is imperative they take advice and acquire representation.

Businesses should use their Disciplinary Procedure to improve the behaviour or performance of their people, so do not assume the worst and DO NOT react aggressively.

Redundancy

Redundancy is a potentially fair reason to dismiss people from employment. In a situation in which a business has completely failed and all employees lose their jobs there is less to debate. There should have been on-going consultation providing some forewarning but this frequently is not the case. At least in this scenario nobody is selected for redundancy, with the possible associated feelings of rejection.

More frequently organisations look to reduce the numbers of staff. This is given various names, like;

> Downsizing
> Rightsizing
> Manpower Management
> Re-structuring
> Re-organising

Redundancy means some people losing their job. There has to be a fair, objective and rigorous process to carry out a redundancy, including a method of selection which ensures there is no discrimination.

If you are faced by this prospect, it is crucial professional advice is sought. Many businesses do not do this process well, even some which have been given guidance.

An example basic re-organisation model for the business to adopt should include the stages outlined on the next four pages. There are basic requirements for the process to be adequately met. The organisation's management must;

- Give reasons for redundancies
- Give notice and carry out meaningful consultations
- State the number of people to be made redundant, the mechanisms for selection and the payments which will be made

Example re-structuring process model

1   Definition

        The organisation sets the affordable budget, describes its priorities and activities.

2   Legal Requirements

        The law is constantly changing either through statute or due to case law (interpretations of the law by the courts). The organisation reviews the legislation and ensures its policies and procedures fully comply.

3   Communication

        Whilst recognising there will be commercial and individual sensitivities, it is incumbent on the business to be as transparent and detailed as possible.

4   Commit to, and achieve, equity and fairness.

        Open communication will ensure this is done, which will help everybody involved (including people not directly affected)

5   Review of the current organisation

- Against budget
- In context of existing requirements and initiatives planned in next 12 months or longer
- Bottom up—ensure enough people remain on the ground to do the work and interface with the public. Overlay this with management, not the other way around.
- Identifies that which doesn't need to be done
- Highlights the needs for improved infrastructure. Considers the impact of systems and any other improvements

6   Define Organisation needs
- Skills/knowledge/expertise
- Layers of management
- Create the new structure

7   Describe the parameters for selection
- SKILLS being paramount
- Service
- Selection Pools (groups from which to select)
- Disciplinary Record
- Performance (e.g. appraisals)
- Personal traits and characteristics

N.B. All evaluations should be reviewed to ensure the evaluation is fair, without bias and meets the criteria (eliminates the possible blue-eyed boy syndrome prevailing).

All assessors MUST be fully trained

8   Process enactment—see next page

Process enactment

There must be consultation. If there are recognised Trade Unions, it will be clear with whom this should occur. If it is proposed to make more than twenty people redundant, and there is no recognised arrangement with a TU, employee representatives must be consulted. If there is no existing forum, representatives would need to be elected. If the number to lose their jobs is twenty or less there must be individual consultation with everyone affected.

Consultation does not mean reaching consensus or agreement but it does need to be meaningful.

If more than twenty redundancies are expected the first date anyone can be compelled to leave is thirty days after the consultation process begins, not merely after any initial general communication was issued. This rises to ninety days for one hundred or more job losses.

Consultation

Should include information regarding;

State of the business

Potential impact—redundancies, short time working, shift changes, plant closures, pay reductions

Timescales

Actions to offset redundancies

Selection mechanisms

Selection pools (groups from which redundancies will be made)

Redundancy pay

The whole workforce should be made aware of all proposals. Communication is crucial to the transparency of the process and confidence it is being carried out professionally and objectively.

Headcount reduction

It may seem obvious to say a redundancy should end in a loss of jobs but there are complications. The exercise must not be an excuse to get rid of someone whose face doesn't fit. However, it is very possible for an individual to be displaced from their job and replaced by a colleague, with the job loss elsewhere. This does require a robust selection process.

There may even be recruitment into the company at the same time. This may be to bring in new skills, may reflect a new business direction or be at a different location.

A displaced person may be offered an alternative job. Very careful thought should be given before rejecting this option. It is possible to be considered to have resigned. There is a four week trial period. Unless there are profound reasons to reject the offer it is sensible to consider the alternative job thoroughly.

Redundancy pay

There are three elements;

1 Statutory Redundancy Pay (tax free and compulsory)
2 Pay-in-lieu of contractual notice (taxable and unlimited)
3 Ex-gratia payment made by the organisation in recognition of people's contribution and to ease the pain of the outcome. This is a potential subject for the consultation (tax free)

The Statutory Redundancy amount is legally defined;

> The maximum is twenty years' service—the final twenty if it is more than that.

> Each year accrues 1.5 weeks' pay for years worked from 41 years old, 1 week for time worked between 22 and 40, and 0.5 weeks for ages 18 to 21

> There is a maximum payment for each accrued week

Statutory redundancy pay example

A person is 50 years of age, with 20 completed years of service, salary £25000 per annum at a time the maximum payment is £400;

10 years' service whilst 41 or older x 1.5 weeks plus

10 years' service whilst younger than 41 x 1 week
Therefore;

$(10 \times 1.5) + (10 \times 1) \times £400 = £10000$

If the individual's pay varies week-by-week a 12 week average is taken.

Expenses owed, holiday pay and any other monies due have to be paid as well.

Additional points

If a release payment is negotiated the person may be required to sign a Compromise Agreement. In doing this the rights to claim Unfair Dismissal will be given up, as well as other claims against the company. Breaches of health and safety laws may be separated from this release of corporate liability.

Do not be surprised if the company immediately blocks everyone who is displaced from accessing the IT systems. Sadly, there are numerous examples of stupid behaviour by emotional people. Even loyal and sensible people have been known to do unfortunate things. It is seen as a better business practice to consistently block everyone's access rather than regret the damage that occurs.

Affected people are allowed to have reasonable time off to commence their job hunt activities such as to attend an interview or to find training.

Sometimes good organisations provide outplacement support, to assist redundant people to job hunt or find alternatives.

The final letter confirming the termination of employment must include the right of appeal to a more senior manager, who has the authority to overturn the original decision.

Displaced employees may;

- Be expected to work their notice
- Be placed on garden leave (not expected to attend work)
- Be expected to come to work but to focus on job hunt whilst being available to be involved in projects
- Be made redundant immediately

Pre-announcement activities

Even before decisions regarding the names of the people to be made redundant are revealed it may be sensible for you to take some pre-emptive actions, just in case;

Make yourself aware of everything that is going on

Know your rights

Be attentive and question in the correct manner

Mentally attune—this is a time to adapt psychologically

Consider other areas of the organisation in which you could or would like to work

Talk to your partner. Share the burden because they will find out anyway. In this world of instant communication it is very unlikely even a small manpower reduction exercise will remain a secret.

Do not give the impression of acceptance—it could well become a self-fulfilling prophecy. If it is what you want, possibly because of a desire to take early retirement or start up on your own, talk to your manager. It could be a win-win situation.

Find evidence—appraisals, awards, certificates, letters of commendation or training and education qualifications

Dust off the Curriculum Vitae (CV) and commence contingency planning

Remind yourself of your responsibilities and, most importantly, your achievements. What are your transferrable skills?

DO NOT mess up projects or sabotage the business. You are better than that, you don't want to burn bridges, it may lead to dismissal without payment and you would be hurting friends and colleagues.

Notes

Chapter 2

Emotional reactions

Everyone feels pain—it is how it is channelled that matters

The shock of redundancy

The decision to terminate employment will be communicated in a formal meeting. Everybody should take a Trade Union representative or colleague to the meeting, even if it is merely to take notes and witness the exchange. It is likely there will be two people from the company, who ought to be professional. Hopefully, no-one will say inane and inappropriate things like, "I know how you feel", "I was made to do this" or "I am hurting more than you are".

The most common first reaction is shock, even if the person is expecting the news. At this moment the recipient of the information typically stops listening, thoughts begin to race and time freezes.

The best course of action is to take any papers and letters, and leave the meeting. The managers may suggest you go home. Take the offer. They may insist everyone goes home. Of course, one course of action for the company is to terminate employment immediately but the right of appeal will remain.

Do not get into an argument or express any opinions. The proper place to raise issues is at an appeal. If you feel there may be reasons for an Unfair Dismissal claim at Industrial Tribunal you must appeal.

An appeal against redundancy can be because of procedural mistakes or omissions, because there are factual errors, wrongful selection or there is alleged discrimination. You will be expected to put forward a cogent argument, with available evidence, to try to reverse the original decision.

After departure from employment

To a lesser or greater degree there will be feelings which are like those after a death;

Shock—how can this have happened? Why me?

Bargaining—if I promise to do better can I stay? I will take a pay cut if I can keep my job

Denial and disbelief—surely someone will come along and say it has all been a mistake and I can have my old job back. Numbness and confusion will pervade.

Anger and sadness—this is unfair and someone should pay. Now I may lose my house, family, friends and standard of living.

Acceptance—there is a life still to be lived and people to love.

It is not unnatural to blame;

The management who failed to see how valuable I am and how much better I am than other people; they tried to stitch me up.

My colleagues who plotted against me; they took credit for my efforts; they looked after themselves.

Yourself as you didn't do enough; you didn't display your talents properly; you accepted the promotion which made you vulnerable.

One of the key issues will be personal honesty but rational honesty. Do not attempt to worry about fault. This is the beginning of the process to describe the rest of your life. Planning starts now.

How might it be displayed physically?

There will be increased stress and in some cases it may show as;

Loss of sleep
Lethargy
Fatigue
Increased blood pressure
More frequent bouts of illness
Weight loss and appetite suppression
Heavier drinking
Lack of concentration
Crying
Avoiding friends and family

What is lost? Everyone will feel some loss, perhaps;

Prestige	Security
Income	Purpose
Meaning	Affiliation
Friendship	Structure
Certainty	Identity
Respect	Attachment

BUT also it may mean losing employment which was, if honest;

Boring	Physically demanding
Under paid	Unchallenging
Repetitive	Always under threat
Diminishing	Threatening

What do we want to find?

Something which is more;

Challenging
Appropriate
Fun
Satisfying
Worthy
Highly paid
Motivating
Pleasant
Respected

Notes

Chapter 3

Early days activities

There is no time like the present

Your job now is to find a job or an alternative.

Apply yourself to this task as professionally as any other task or project in your life. It is not something to give a couple of hours' attention each day. It matters more than anything else at this time and you are answerable to your family and yourself.

Be open and honest, especially with the ones you love and love you. There are numerous examples of redundant people pretending there are no problems; still leaving for work at the same time; filling their days somehow; arriving home at the normal time; spending their life savings and going into significant debt.

Whilst a trouble shared is not literally a trouble halved, it does allow others to support, help and contribute ideas. This is not a time for false pride or fear. Like all problems, there are solutions and you need to find one quickly.

Day One

Get up early—this is a busy day and slothing in bed cannot help. This is the first day of the rest of your life. Eat breakfast. It is easy at this point to panic about money and cut costs everywhere. Your health is vital and you need to be energetic all day.

Visit Jobcenter Plus. This will give you an immediate sense of purpose. Register your unemployment (they may give you an appointment). Ask, what assistance is available? Ask, what are you entitled to receive? Ask, what advice is there?

Note the style is to ask open questions. It seems government officials are trained to answer the question asked. So, if you ask, "Am I entitled to Unemployment Benefit?" you will be given a simple yes or no reply. Too many of them will not develop the thought to say, "Yes and other benefits as well". They are decent people but are busy.

Remembering at this stage you are gathering information it is worth talking to other people and organisations such as Citizens Advice Bureau, Trade Union and professional advisors.

If you haven't completed the activities at your (ex) employer make sure it is done;

- *Appeal if you intend to do so*
- *Ask for a detailed briefing of the reasons for selection*
- *Ask what support is available, such as outplacement (if it is, use it fully)*
- *Collect personal belongings*
- *Find out the names of other people affected. Potentially, there is a support group to be formed. Note contact details—customers, suppliers, colleagues*
- *Ask for a reference and ensure your P45 will follow*

Negotiate

The consultation may have defined redundancy payments. However, it may be possible to negotiate the release package.

This could be broader than money but the ex-gratia segment is very flexible. If you have had a company car, laptop or pension arrangement, compensation for them should be debated. If there is no discretionary amount added to the base package, do not sign a Compromise Agreement.

The notice period is a variable. It is worth seeking to extend this element, although it is the taxable portion of the overall amount.

If outplacement support isn't immediately offered, it too may be negotiated into the final settlement. Professional assistance is likely to shorten the time it takes to successfully resolve this personal predicament.

Back at home

List out financial commitments, for example;

-   mortgage or rent
-   insurance
-   pensions
-   council tax
-   credit cards

What income is there? Partner's job, pension, investments . . .

Do you have mortgage insurance?

Does any action need to be taken immediately? Stopping proposed expenditure?

The issue is cash flow. How quickly will money run out if no actions are taken? Make an appointment to see the bank manager. Banks don't like surprises, so ask for help.

At least as important as money is the support for each other. The other family members are as worried as you and they are feeling impotent. You will find the job, they can only give you emotional backing.

Everyone needs to recognise things will change, especially in the short term. Adjustments will be made but it is, hopefully, only for a while. The worst thing would be additional pressure from unsupportive family and friends.

Emotions are still raw. Don't suppress them; channel them.

Start your research. This will be constrained if you do not have access to the internet. The library and friends can assist but as most things are done on-line it may be a worthwhile investment. Certainly, if you have access, do not see its removal as a potential saving.

Day 2

Draft a CV—see chapter 5

Make lists of friends and contacts

Search for helpful websites

Consider the variables;

Location—can you move home or commute?

Salary—what do you want and what is the minimum you could accept?

What are the practical implications for the family?

Are there carer issues?

What can you really not leave or cease?

Are there industries or companies for which you could not work?

Days 3 to 7

Develop the CV

Have the CV critiqued (do not send off the CV until it is refined)

Search for vacancies—see chapter 5

Meet people and be active

> Ex-colleagues
>
> Any advisors
>
> Bank manager
>
> Agencies—see chapter 5

Be wary of loan sharks and others who absolutely do not have your best interests on their list of priorities

Prepare for your appeal if there is to be one

Personal disciplines

For all of the things you do maintain an accurate and complete record such as, contacts, applications, replies and interviews. Make notes of any feedback and points of improvement you have recognised. This is not a time for your ego to dominate but for humility, inquisitiveness and adaptability. These need to be balanced with an air of confidence.

When attending any event dress smartly. You never know who may be highly influential, who may know someone with an opportunity or can give you direction. Make an impact and always be prepared to impress.

Never attend a meeting underprepared. Complacency and overconfidence are enemies of successful job search. The more you know and the more you have thought about the issues, the more likely you are to reach your goal of employment.

Notes

Chapter 4

Being thoughtful

Knowing yourself and your real employment desires

Influence the things YOU can control

Don't fret about the items over which you can have no power

Take responsibility for your life and job hunt

Work at the elements of your job search performance

Be detail conscious

Be proactive

Think of people from whom you can take advice and guidance

You decide on the advice you take

You will determine the amount of effort you put into your job hunt

Control—

The amount you spend

Your appearance

Your preparation

The time you get up in the morning

The amount you drink and eat

Your health and fitness—this is a chance to get yourself much fitter. Walking, for example, gives great thinking and preparation time.

The time you commit to considering the options which may become available

Self-Assessment

Be honest with yourself;

Was I worth the money?

Did I do just enough to survive?

Was I a positive influence?

Was I scared of losing my job and did it affect my performance?

Was I really first division?

Why was I selected?

Was I flexible, adaptable, committed, supportive, productive, empathetic, open, communicative, creative, innovative, detailed, quality conscious, enthusiastic, focused, positive, skilled or motivated? Or should I have been?

On a scale of 0-10 how would I rate myself? How easily could that be much higher?

What are your passions and drivers?

Are you inspired by, for example?

Intellectual pursuits
Physical work
Beauty
Emotions
Ethics
Compassion and justice
Entertainment
Materialism
The environment

How could these translate into employment preferences?

Do a SWOT analysis

Strengths
Skills
Relationships
Experience
Maturity
Personal traits
Positivity

Weaknesses
Redundant skills
Insularity
Negativity
Employment record
Reliance on others
Uncertainty

Opportunities
Fundamental review
Time
Relieve pressures
New start
New friends
Improved relationships

Threats
Debts
Divorce or break-up
Mortgage
Emotional strangulation
Age
Under expectation

These are indicative headings. Personal honesty is of paramount importance for this to be a valuable exercise.

Breaking the mental shackles

Do you assume you;

Can only have a poorly paid job?

Can't improve upon your current skills?

Won't earn enough to enjoy great experiences?

Must live in the same area?

Can't make new friends?

Cannot be successful?

Must make do with that which you have?

Can't live in a bigger house?

Aren't admired by other people?

Can only take the line of least resistance?

Imagine

What is your dream job?

What do you really want to do?

In which sector would you LOVE to work?

If you had the choice of any job which would it be and why?

How can you remove your limitations?

With whom would you like to work?

If you could do a job for a day which one would it be? Why not for life?

Where would you love to live?

How would you know if you are happy?

What would make your family happy?

The nature of work

We live in an ever evolving world. Technology is developing at an incredible speed. Maybe it is revolution rather than evolution. For everyone there is a major implicit challenge;

For example;

The top ten jobs in the eyes of 18 years old school leavers today didn't exist five years ago

There are 50 graduates applying for every vacancy

School leavers are expected to have, on average, between 10 and 14 jobs by the time they are 38 years old

The UK manufacturing sector is still shrinking and service industries are attempting to fill the void

The job hunter needs to think TIRELESS(LY)

Traits   What characteristics do you want in an employer? Balance your aspirations with the reality of the businesses under consideration

Individuality   Are you going to be able to express yourself but fit into the new culture?

Rewards   Do you know what you want, will accept?

Environment   Are you prepared to work the hours/shifts and in the style of a workplace?

Location   Is the geography acceptable? Can you commute?

Excitement   Is this going to inspire you?

Skills   Do you have the skills? Can you acquire them?

Sector   Is this an industry, company or product to which is acceptable or to which you can relate?

Consider the variables of work

Full-time or part-time

Permanent/interim/temporary

Fixed term contract?

Portfolio work (a number of part-time jobs)

Local employer/commute/travel/work away from home/work from home/ work from a local office remote from the employer/work on the road

Employed or self-employed

Start times/shift patterns

Overtime ramifications

Weekend work

Sectors/industries

Brands/products/companies

When do they want you to start? Do you need a sabbatical?

What help do you need?

Personal coaching?

A career coach?

A confidante?

A base?

A computer and internet connection?

Love and support?

Reassurance?

Space?

Time?

Advice?

Training?

Interrogative pronouns

A helpful poem to aid thinking and questioning is;

I keep six honest serving men
(They taught me all I know)
Their names are: What and Why and When
And How and Where and Who

Rudyard Kipling

Notes

Chapter 5

Job search processes

Nobody is coming to find you

Practical issues in job search

You have given some real thought to the situation in which you find yourself and what you would like life to look like in the near future. Now it is time to apply this thinking to the difficult task of finding a job.

How long will it take to find a job? There is research which over-simplifies the answer to this question. It says the average time is one month for each £10000 of the aspirational salary. So, a £50000 job takes 5 months to acquire. This is a basic arithmetic mean and is complicated by other factors such as age, personal flexibility, narrow employer criteria and the individuals' state of mind.

Whilst we look at the impact of age in Chapter 8 it is worth acknowledging it may be a factor. This reflects on the opportunities for younger and older job searchers.

Employers may be biased against people unemployed for over six months or so. Be able to rebut this with evidence such as active voluntary work. Some people have the protection of a year's mortgage insurance cover which makes it difficult financially to take a more lowly-paid job until it expires.

Without question the fundamental determining factor is personal attitude. Therefore, being in a positive frame of mind is absolutely crucial. Easily said but burdened by unemployment and its ramifications, not easy to achieve.

Seek assistance and guidance if it is too difficult.

Finding vacancies

It is perhaps a surprise truism that there are thousands of vacant jobs, even in economically suppressed times. The trick is finding them. Of course, if you want a £50000 job at the end of your home road, doing exactly what you want, it may be more problematic.

So where can these vacancies be found? A recurring theme of this short book is it will take time, thought and a little ingenuity.

The possibilities we are now going to consider are not exhaustive but are typical. There are amazing stories of coincidence and luck which have transformed the lives of people, giving them a job, hope and security. It is time for you to make your own luck through diligence and application.

A question you may ask is "For how many jobs should I apply?" There is no correct answer but you need to ensure they are all relevant and you can keep track.

It may take ten applications to gain one interview and ten interviews to attract one offer but this will vary according to level, salary, industry and most importantly the quality of your job search competence.

Sources

<u>Jobcentre Plus (JCP)</u> or whatever name it is operating as.

You are attending the job centre anyway, so look at the possibilities. It is no longer a big board with handwritten jobs just from the immediate vicinity. There are touchscreens which allow you to access all vacancies notified throughout the country.

There are weaknesses to JCP and no single source should be relied on. For example;

- A large number of vacancies are not given to it
- Few senior positions are notified to JCP
- Everyone can see the jobs and it is exceedingly competitive

Newspapers

Advertising in papers is expensive, so many vacancies are not published. It is worth doing research to identify which papers feature which disciplines and on which days. Local papers can be a real hotchpotch and careful reading is needed. Again there will be thousands of people seeing these adverts and, consequently, it will be a highly competitive market. Someone will get the job; why can't it be you?

Journals

The advantage of trade magazines is the focus they bring. If you are in Human Resources, the journal People Management only has HR jobs displayed. Of course, all HR people know this and the opposition is well qualified.

Some of these publications are for members of the respective institutes only and this can inhibit people considering a radical change of career.

Institutes and Trade bodies

If access is limited to the journals contact the organisation directly. In this example, if you are thinking about a career in HR, the relevant body (Chartered Institute of Personnel and Development) will readily give advice, including regarding training and qualifications.

Friends

This is not a time to be shy. There is no stigma attached to being unemployed. It is a sad fact of everyday life for millions. Some people may be embarrassed by your situation but help them deal with it by being positive and optimistic. The question is rarely, "Have you got a job for me?" It is, "Do you know of any vacancies or of people whom could assist me?" There is no pressure on them but they would love to be able to help. Once your position is widely known you will be surprised about the number of offers of assistance you will receive.

Contacts

Through work and social situations you have come into contact with scores or hundreds of people. In a discerning way, make a list of people with whom you have had a positive interaction. Who have you impressed? Who knows about your capabilities? Do not be shy. It is time to be pleasantly assertive. Previous bosses are an excellent prospect. After all they know you well and trust you. Where are they now? Even your last manager may also have been made redundant. Has this person found employment and is there a slot available for you?

Direct approaches

If you are going to write to companies unsolicited, there are some things you must do;

Be sure you are interested in the company

Send it to a named person, preferably the Managing Director or someone in Human Resources

Keep it short, accurate and well presented. Make it easy for the recipient to like your approach.

Cold Calling

If you think a business has opportunities it may be worth visiting. However, you must know the name of a relevant person and attend well presented.

Direct letters and visits are very rarely successful. They can infer desperation and an inability to acquire a job due to inferior skills or capabilities. This is a disproportionate amount of effort for little prospect of a good outcome. Use time wisely.

Voluntary organisations

Occasionally, a voluntary role becomes a paid one. More importantly, doing voluntary or charitable work impresses on a CV, gives personal credibility and satisfaction, and new skills are often acquired.

Re-education

Going onto a training or educational programme may also bring the students into contact with potential employers. Therefore, it is very important to also impress the tutors with punctuality, presentation and attitude, as well as academic diligence.

Social Media

These are mechanisms for you to contact friends and colleagues. Some are more effective, such as Linkedin, but there may be the one person needing someone amongst your friends on Facebook, Twitter or Friends Reunited. Don't be shy.

One caveat to remember about social media is companies thinking of hiring staff now frequently check the content of these on-line pages. Be careful what you say and how you say it.

The internet

There are hundreds of websites advertising jobs. This is an exceedingly important area for you to focus your efforts. Research into these links can provide you with a tremendous source of vacancies. Some are specialist but many seek to show jobs across many disciplines and industries.

Do not pursue any website which wants you to give them money.

Only contact them when your CV is fit-for-purpose.

Recognise there will be little personal attention unless you begin a conversation with a potential employer or the agency sees you as a realistic candidate for an available role.

Many on-line agencies will send you hundreds of vacancies once you have registered. This can be frustrating if you haven't defined clearly enough your preferences. They may also send you job hunt tips (but be discerning). Some will offer to improve your CV—check immediately if there is a cost to you. How else will they make their money?

Be wary but this is a great potential source. Be clear about your ambitions and closely define the jobs in which you are interested. Spend time delving into the websites and what they can offer you.

The final group of organisations we are going to discuss are;

<u>Employment agencies</u>

Most have a small number of specialisms which help you concentrate on those most relevant. Many companies give their vacancies to agencies because they then receive a list of candidates perceived to be appropriate. The initial shift of CV's and application forms is undertaken remote to the business. Given some vacancies attract hundreds of applications this isn't surprising.

It is important to remember agencies are not really interested in who gets the job as long as someone they have proffered does. Then they get paid. To many agencies you are no more than a product to sell. Every one of them will tell you how important you are but they say it to all of the other people registered with them and it will be a very large number. There may be little regular contact unless it suits them. Don't expect to enjoy a developing relationship. It isn't without precedent for an agency to ring to ask if you are interested in a job, excite you with tales of your suitability and no further contact is ever made. It is a waste of time for them to tell people not on the interview list, as the next assignment (and fee) awaits their attention. It is fundamentally rude but acknowledged as typical. The acting profession operates in very much the same manner. Move on.

Be very circumspect about using agencies which send your CV to businesses on a speculative basis. Very few lead to an appointment. Most are filed in the wastepaper bin or instantly deleted from the inbox. Agencies like this get a bad reputation and their candidates are the victims. Do the research; which of your friends has had success through an agency? Are any of your contacts responsible for hiring and which agencies do they use?

Ask the agency if it is given exclusive rights to fill vacancies? What is its success rate?

Focus your time and energy in the correct places.

For more senior roles, businesses employ executive recruitment companies. These people do the correct things. They match people and job; they prepare the company to receive good candidates; they communicate fully with the candidates; they treat everyone in the process professionally. They are selling but repeat business comes from fulfilling the role effectively.

The Curriculum Vitae (CV)

Our view is the CV has a number of purposes;

It is, as every book will tell you, to acquire an interview or movement to the next stage of the process.

However, its submission also sets part of the agenda for any subsequent interview. Do not underestimate this. Of course, the immediate aim is to be invited to interview but it is the next stages which will get you the job. The CV will not get you a job but it can lose you any chance you may have had.

The CV is your first chance to make a positive impression and we all know you only have one chance to make a first impression. It is a great opportunity to display your strengths and abilities.

You are literally attempting to be the author of your own (career) destiny.

The review of a CV

It is important to assume the CV you submit is one of hundreds that will need to be sifted through by the agency or employer. None of them will be read thoroughly at this juncture. It must make an impact. If it looks tatty, poorly presented and amateurish it will fail immediately.

Your CV must make the key points visibly. It must scream this person is worth spending more time under review. The majority of CV's will be rejected at this first sift stage, so yours has to emphasise your match to the job requirements, your skills and qualifications, and your relevant achievements. Proud as you are about the MBE Her Majesty has given you or the voluntary work you do, these are less relevant at this point.

The depth of your personal qualities will begin to permeate the recruiters conscience at second sift stage. The deadwood is out and a "long list" needs to be produced. Now your CV needs to demonstrate the depth and substance of your career and potential.

Today most submissions are made electronically but if you need to send a paper form ensure it goes on decent quality paper. It ought to go without saying that it should be grammatically correct and the spelling perfect. Sadly, even in the days of spellcheck CV's are sent with numerous errors. They may be automatically dismissed. Many people feel this is unjust and good candidates are excluded. Probably true but remember the volume of CV's being read and the abundance of good candidates who are demonstrating their attention to detail and enthusiasm for the chance to impress. It is a great idea to have a trusted friend read, critique and check the CV before it is sent anywhere. Please ensure that spellcheck is set to English UK and not USA.

If the CV is requested electronically it may be sifted, in the first instance, by an automatic tracking system. This is even more likely for an on-line application form.

It is crucial you use the key words which will trigger with the system. Remember a human being will not read your deft prose at this stage. Read the advertisement or job profile if one is available and use the obvious leads.

If it is an engineering role explicitly say engineer, rather than the obscure job title you once enjoyed. If it seeks graduates, and you are one, write BSc, BA, MSc or as appropriate. For production jobs include words like delivery, quality and process improvement.

This can be the easiest element of the whole process.

Rules for the CV

DO NOT lie or embellish. Even if it gets you to interview you will be found out and your chance of success disappears instantly. It is not true that everyone lies on the CV. Why take a chance? Why undermine yourself? Why lie? It merely demonstrates you are unprincipled.

Do not leave gaps in your history as people may make unfounded assumptions.

Be accurate and brief.

Be relevant. Frustrating as it may feel, you may well need to adapt your CV to the description of the job and the industry.

Include the key information.

Have different CV's for permanent or temporary/ interim roles. The latter requires a greater emphasis on successful projects and the ability to immediately make an impact.

Without using very small font keep it to two pages.

CV structures

If you are applying for jobs in the same type of work as you have been doing the format might be;

Name and contact details

Personal profile which headlines background and strengths

Employment history

Achievements and emphasises successful delivery

Qualifications and memberships

Education and training

Additional supporting information

Personal data including impressive interests

If you are seeking to change industries or the type of role you want to perform it will be appropriate to change some of the emphases and the order in the presentation;

Name and contact details

Personal profile—tweaked for the vacancy

Achievements—particularly those which support this application

Skills and abilities—highlighting the relevant ones to this sought change of direction

Employment—bringing out relevant projects and demonstrating flexibility

Qualifications and memberships

Education and training

Additional supporting information

Personal data

The CV for temporary or interim roles may look different again;

Name and contact details

Personal profile—tweaked for the vacancy

Achievements—particularly those which support this application

Skills and abilities—highlighting the relevant ones to this type of contract

Recent clients or employers, if possible

The nature of assignments

Qualifications and memberships

Education and training

Additional supporting information

Personal data

Items not to be included in a CV

Current or last salary

Reasons for leaving jobs

Health

Referees—just say available on request

Too much detail—if you have twenty years' experience the detail of GCSE's is not going to influence the decision to grant an interview.

Optional topics to consider are;

Age—you may choose to place it at the end rather than exclude it. Your CV will give clues anyway and it eliminates the doubt you forgot to include it.

Marital status

Details regarding children

Driving licence unless it is crucial to the prospective role

Personal profile

Whilst it appears first on the CV it may be better to write it last, so it reflects the body of the content. It is impossible to generalise as each of us is different. You want to show the positives;

Experienced, energetic, diligent, hardworking, successful, flexible

Skilled, knowledgeable, creative, innovative

Team player, problem solver, deliverer

Breadth or depth of background

Leadership qualities, communication capabilities

It should only be one or two sentences to set the scene which encourages the reader to continue to see the evidence. If you were in one job for a long time emphasise loyalty, tenacity and commitment. If you have had a number of jobs for a short time the key words may be energetic, ambitious, flexible and adaptable.

Body of the contents

Employment;

Employer

Job title

Achievements (e.g. implemented a new quality system by benchmarking Japanese companies. State what before how)

Responsibilities (not just a list of day-to-day activities but things for which you are or were accountable such as production of high quality products to given targets)

Give greater prominence to most recent jobs and merely mention those from the distant past if your career is long. If you are relatively inexperienced the early career will be the most recent positions.

Qualifications and memberships

If you don't have any omit this section. However, if you have a degree (or more) this is the key level. Do not add detail regarding the number or grade of GCSE's, as a degree clearly demonstrates the capacity to pass lower level courses.

Don't reveal you only got a third class degree or, if true, do ensure the fact you gained a first class honours degree is unmissable.

If you don't have a degree, reflect the highest level achieved such as an HND, A levels or GCSE's

It is highly relevant to state any membership of institutes even if not directly relevant to the job application. Letters after the name have cachet. Membership of social clubs would come elsewhere.

Training

Most people have attended numerous training courses. For the CV it is necessary to pick the important ones. Consider if they;

Are certificated or licensed

Are quality biased

Help problem solving

Are relevant to the job being sought

Relate to Health and Safety

Give flexibility (e.g. HGV licence when applying for general production operative role)

IT courses—if you are proficient say so

Do not list scores of one day programmes which have tenuous value.

Personal details

In this section you may include;

Interests—do not create a long list; do not say socialising, drinking, watching TV or relaxing. Impress with current affairs, travel, sport, voluntary work or local history. Remember whatever you put down will have to be substantiated at interview. It must be true and have depth.

Address

Age, if you want to reveal it or think it will give you an advantage.

Marital status, if you choose to state it. Being married may, for example, give the recruiters a sense of your maturity and responsibility

Anything else which may impress e.g. MBE, represented the country at a sport, published author

Personal attributes

What characteristics do companies want to recruit and how else can they be displayed?

Employers frequently describe preferred staff as being, for example, team players, loyal, flexible, self-starters, creative or detail-conscious. It may seem daunting thinking how to demonstrate any of these traits. We would ask you to consider evidence from non-work activities as well. Too many people fail to see the value of other interests.

Have you organised a wedding? List the skills needed to do that well.

Do you run a football team or youth club? This is leadership in action

Are you a parent governor at a school? This is a role with responsibilities and complexity

Style for the CV

Use active verbs like; achieved, designed, implemented, delivered, validated, managed, produced, recruited.

Write in the third person rather than say "I" repeatedly. For example, do write, "An experienced lathe operator" instead of, "I can operate a lathe".

Choose a font and size which are easy to read.

Less is more. You can go into the detail at interview.

Be clear and simple, to appeal to the very busy readers.

Well organised and linked together.

Emphasise achievements rather than listing the minutiae of the roles.

You are starting to build a relationship, so try to convey the fact they can trust you.

Application forms

Frequently companies require candidates to complete application forms rather than accept CV's. This is for their benefit rather than yours but with a little thought you can use it to best advantage.

Why do companies use application forms?

-   Ensures consistency and fairness
-   Aids equal opportunity monitoring (in best practice the page for personal details will be detachable to allow the decision maker to do so without any possible inference of bias)
-   It will collect information which may be omitted from a CV
-   It makes the initial sift easier and aid the comparison of key criteria

Completing an application form

How to do it

- Make a copy of the form to complete as a draft. This will give you a sense of the space and plan your answers ensuring the most important messages are included.
- Read the instructions and follow them.
- Read the form, so you know all of the sections, so you do not repeat yourself, waste space and waste the recruiter's time.
- If it is to be handwritten use black ink or biro (you want to make it easy for the recruiter).

Style

As with the CV, do not lie or embellish. You will be asked to sign to say the information is accurate. Not only may you fail to get a job but you can also be dismissed from it even if you were successful at interview.

- Use examples and emphasise achievements. Accentuate the positives and be careful to avoid negative aspects of your career. Let the form help you to relate your skills and experience to the vacancy.
- Use your CV to prompt your answers. If you have given the appropriate amount of thought and time to it there will be many relevant guidelines. If a CV is requested later there will be consistency.
- Never fill a question box with a phrase like "See CV". If a CV was acceptable there wouldn't be an application form. This may be assumed to be laziness. It will, in all probability, be the end of any chance of progressing through the selection process.
- It may be right to put "not applicable" but do answer every question.

Logistics of completion

- Give yourself plenty of time to fill the form in properly. Draft it, reflect and get someone to critique it. Redo it if necessary. Doing it quickly is not the goal; doing it well is.
- Retain a copy, so that in preparation for an interview you can remind yourself of the detail included.
- Attach an accompanying letter (see the next section)
- Do not fold the form; find an envelope big enough to take it. Do make sure you put an adequate stamp on.

Some of these hints won't apply if the form is completed on-line but the principles will. It is too easy to overlook the need to review, check and edit the content, when the satisfaction of making the application is the press of one button away.

Covering letter

What is the letter trying to achieve?

<u>Context</u>

Create a heading, indicating the vacancy for which you are applying. Not to do so makes you appear amateurish and the process more difficult for the recruiter.

<u>Introduction</u>

Lead into your CV. There must be a desire to read the CV and to want it to be relevant. If the letter is full of waffle and irrelevances the recruiter may just assume this is indicative of the person and by-pass the rest of the application.

<u>Clarify</u>

Demonstrate the appropriateness of your candidacy.

<u>Impact</u>

Signal you are worth the time for full consideration.

The same rules apply to a letter as to the CV;

Check all spelling and grammar
Be brief (one page for the letter)
Be professional

You are endeavouring to show why you should be considered, how you fit the specification and what you have to offer.

Make life easy for the recruiter by making the obvious decision the one to move your application to the second stage.

One small warning—do not use a silly or frivolous email address such as

john.smith@themadhouse.com
jane.smith@mickeymouse.co.uk

It cannot be an aide to serious job hunting.

Notes

Chapter 6

Selection processes

*Methods of torture
(or at least it can feel like it
for the unprepared)*

What processes might be used?

It is too easy to assume that there will be one or more interviews, possibly with increasingly senior people; or first there will be an interview with Human Resources to further sift the candidates, followed by the departmental management. Often this will be the case but increasingly candidates need to be prepared for other aspects and techniques.

<u>Interviews</u>

These will be addressed in greater detail in the next chapter but it is worth noting there are different types including, as a preliminary stage, a telephone interview or conversation by video conference. This saves everyone a lot of time and effort. Candidates, for whom the reality of success is less likely, can be eliminated early.

Psychometrics

Many organisations use this type of approach to see if people are intelligent and have the personality to work in the discipline. These tests should never be taken in isolation but may be by some businesses. Psychometric tests will never get you the job but can exclude you from it. There is no true way to "cheat", to convey the desired impression. Firstly, you don't know what is being sought and secondly you should always be yourself. Why fight for a job for which you are unsuited?

Assessment Centres

These are typically used for senior roles or specialisms such as sales or supervision.

They may last for two days, have overnight tasks and include a range of exercises. There may well be one or more interviews, role plays, written papers and presentations.

Assessment Centres are designed to test a range of abilities, to pressurise and to gain a much broader insight to the individual. It may be preceded by Psychometric Tests as well.

Things to remember;

Whatever is said to the contrary by the assessors, everything is monitored and noted. Any conversation at, for example, a meal which seems relaxed and pleasant will be assessed and put into the overall review. Do not become paranoid but do keep your concentration. You are there to create a positive impression, not to make friends or entertain assessors and fellow candidates.

No single exercise is likely to be terminal. Not performing too well in a presentation is not the end of your chances; assuming you are finished and being uncommitted in the other elements will ensure failure.

It is a competitive situation. There may be several people going for one job. However, seeking to eliminate the opposition by politics or stealth will reflect on you, not them. Companies do not preach the need for team players and then recruit loners. Demonstrate how much you want to work with other people and how well you do it.

Do not sit back and assume the assessors will be able to see your innate talents. Give them the evidence. Participate and contribute to discussions and situations. This does not mean behaving falsely, as if you are always the centre of attention. Be yourself but be involved.

If there is an overnight stay with work to do, don't stay up all night drinking with the assessors even if you can do it and complete the work. It is not a freebie; it is the gateway to your next career move.

However relaxed you become, NEVER swear and do not join in irrelevant banter. Be professional, personable and credible.

Graphology

Even today, some less enlightened companies use analysis of handwriting as a tool for evaluation. You cannot fudge this but why would you want to work for this company anyway? It is the same with astrology and some other non-scientific ideas. They would be more accurate tossing a coin. Professional organisations use professional techniques.

Trials

There is no better mechanism for all concerned than doing the job. Inevitably, any offer of a trial will be at the end of a selection process. For the candidate, if it is logistically feasible, this gives a chance to impress and to find out if the role and the business are acceptable to them. If a trial is offered it is fundamental to know on what basis, what is expected and the criteria for success or failure. It needs to be more than, "We will see how it goes".

Notes

Chapter 7

The interview

*Selling the unique product
that is you*

For many employers and candidates this is the critical stage of the whole process and, irrespective of other information provided, it is paramount. This chapter will deal with;

- What is an interview?

- Interviewers

- Practical preparation

- Emotional preparation

- Creating an impression

- Their questions

- Answers

- Your questions

- Personal style

- Post-interview actions

What is an interview?

An interview is, in essence, a formal conversation to establish the suitability of a candidate for an available job. The levels of formality may vary, as might the structure, number of interviewers, the type of location and the length of time and nature of questioning. Even unpaid roles may require an interview.

The interview is the traditional process for making selections, it is the expectation. It has the advantage of being interactive, reactive and multi-dimensional.

It is two-way and gives both parties the chance to assess each other. Do they match the needs and aspirations of each other?

Whilst there is a need for transparency there will be an understandable inclination to display positive traits. The interview allows some investigation of claims and statements made.

The nature of interviews can differ. To discuss a vacancy with an employment agency could easily lead the individual to assume the job is in the bag. They want to keep a broad range of candidates to give themselves the best chance of being paid the commission. Therefore, they need people with an expectation of success.

Telephone interviews are less personal. Not seeing the person at the other end of the phone can be off-putting, even though we all spend a great deal of our lives chatting through this medium. Be very careful not to become too friendly and lose focus. The excellent news is you can have your CV and other information in front of you, without embarrassment. Video conferences are less common and not everyone has access to a computer and camera, although most new laptops have them built-in. If this is a new mechanism for you it is worth practising. Be especially aware to ensure it appears you are concentrating and not glancing off at distractions. Do not have anyone else in the room.

A first face-to-face interview may be to sift candidates and reduce a long list to a shortlist. It may be with someone junior to the final decision maker or with Human Resources. The questions may be more general and the allocated time less but you still have to impress. Conversely, don't leave your "A game" for the next person. This may be it.

Most importantly an interview is your opportunity to sell yourself. The subject about which you truly are an expert is YOU. However, there is too much information, a life's worth. What are the key and relevant messages which will make you a strong runner in this race?

Think clearly about the themes and information which are crucial to create the best perspectives.

Interviewers

Not all interviewers are very good at it, which again creates a chance for you to establish your credibility.

They choose busy venues which may put some people off. So, by keeping your concentration you can differentiate yourself from other candidates.

Poor interviewers allow interruptions, so maintain your focus. If you were in the middle of an answer briefly re-cap and continue. Poor interviewers discuss issues with each other and almost ignore the candidate. You should look interested and keen to address any questions.

Poor interviewers talk a lot more than the interviewee. This allows you to learn a great deal regarding the organisation and the interviewers' thinking.

Poor interviewers ask closed questions like, "Do you agree with me?" and "Have you looked at the company website?"

Good interviewers create the right atmosphere to allow the candidate to demonstrate skills and appropriateness for the job.

They ask questions aimed at finding out more from the other person rather than taking the chance to talk about themselves. However, they will provide an excellent overview of the company, the department and the job.

It is not a matter of tricking the interviewee but probing questions will search for real evidence to support answers.

There will be a balance of friendliness to put the candidate at ease with enough formality to reflect the serious nature of the event.

Good interviewers have excellent judgement and, of course, are able to eliminate weaker candidates.

Practical preparation

Research

The internet allows access to huge amounts of data regarding all aspects of the prospective employer. Names of interviewers can allow investigation through social media and searches. A really good candidate goes deeper than the rest. Who do you know that has detailed knowledge of them? What do the accounts actually tell you? Who are their customers and suppliers?

One quick read of the company website is not research; it is indicating that busking an interview is the preferred approach.

If this is a new industry or sector for you, read and educate yourself. The interviewer knows this is new to you, so impress by your diligence and commitment to learn.

Know the job specification completely, how you meet it and things you want to know about the role in action.

Location

Do you know how to get there? Are you using a car or public transport? Are there any travel problems? Can you do the journey a few days before the appointment? Is your Sat Nav working? How long will it take? What contingency actions can you take?

Detail

Who are the interviewers? Make sure you get the names correct to ensure you don't make the fundamental error of addressing them wrongly.

What time is the meeting? Do not be late. Even if your excuses are legitimate and entirely valid it will create an implied question mark. Possibly unfair but don't take the chance.

What day is the interview? You would not be unique if you turned up a day, week or month out.

Dress

We live in more informal times but do not make the mistake of assuming smart casual is adequate. Dress smartly and impress. Get your clothes ready the day before, polish shoes, iron shirts/blouses, think co-ordination.

Many people believe assessors ought to consider the person in front of them, rather than someone's willingness to comply with hackneyed convention. This may be true but isn't the case in the majority of occasions. Do you want the job or not?

Revise your CV

Amazingly, people attend interviews and cannot remember the detail in their own CV. Learn it thoroughly; the dates, the roles, the achievements, the training programmes. Countless candidates ask the interviewer if they can see their own CV to remind themselves what is in it. Rarely do these people succeed in their application.

Prepare your questions

In far too many interviews the candidate, when asked if there are any questions for the assessors, declines the invitation and says something like, "You have answered all of my questions". This is a massive opportunity missed. Moving to a new job is a very significant act and they don't appear to need more information. It screams to the interviewers that the person has little imagination, has done no research and probably doesn't want this job. It is madness and an abdication of the personal responsibility that successful job hunting demands.

Surely, the research has prompted some concerns or questions;

New markets, new customers, new advertising?

Financial stability, new investments, new products?

There must be more to know about the job. Does the job description really tell all there is to know?

Company principles and ethics? Do they really live them?

Emotional preparation

It may well be a long time since your last interview; it could be twenty years or more. It may be that in this job hunt process the next interview will be the twentieth or more but this could be the one, so be ready mentally.

- Confident in practical preparation

If you have followed the advice regarding practical preparation it will give you confidence. Many of the things which can go wrong are eliminated. You know where you are going. Your appearance is good. You know your CV thoroughly.

- Rehearse possible answers

Some questions are obvious, so prepare good answers. As more interviews are attended themes will emerge, so be ready for them. Ensure your answers display the points you want to get across to the people on the other side of the table.

- Know the reasons you want this job

Why do you want it? If it is desperation or the money do not admit it. Think of better reasons which are credible and ought to be the case. This is a big personal issue. Employment may be with this company for years, so wouldn't it be preferable if it was a good place to work?

- Even if you are unsure it is the job for you, go get it, then it is your decision

The interview will help you decide if this is a job you want. Do not display any indecision. Be confident in the assertion it is the job for you. The aim is to successfully acquire the job and then the decision is yours.

- Focus on the one subject—the interview

When an interview is granted it is in itself a success. However, there is no guarantee of reaching the next stage or an offer.

The next portion of the programme is even trickier. Taking time to write cogently about yourself and career is easier than the pressured situation that is an interview. It is time to get your thinking straight, to apply yourself to doing well and presenting the product that is you to the customers (the assessors).

- Talk to your family or friends

Trust those that love you. Rehearse with them. Accept feedback. Allow your fears or reservations to be discussed. If the words are spoken, it is often the case the concerns are clarified and solutions found. Trust yourself to find the answers to any problems.

- Breathe deeply

As the time of the interview approaches and you sit (nervously) waiting to go in, breathe deeply. Tension can be healthy and helpful as long as it is controlled. Oxygen assists clear thinking.

In a neat folder, it is acceptable to take items to an interview;

Copies of CV for interviewers—rarely needed but a nice touch

The job advertisement

Map and directions

The job specification

Details of referees

Your questions—better to have them written down than forget. It shows thoroughness but if they are memorised it is better.

Diary—another interview may be proposed at this session

Pad and pen

It is a matter of being prepared. If you are early the data is available for a final read through.

Creating an impression

You only get one chance to make a first impression. So your appearance needs to be right. Visit the toilet before entering the room. Not only may this be good thinking anyway but you can check the way you look and be confident. Have you used antiperspirant? Is your personal hygiene fine? Dry your hands in case a company representative meets you as you walk out of the door. Wet hands are not going to create a positive impression.

Shake hands firmly. If typically this is not your style, practise. Again, this may not be fair or right but do you want the job? Many managers state they can make a decision within five minutes of the start of an interview. Whilst this reflects poorly on them, it is the reality. These people spend the next hour confirming the early judgement. There is research which indicates the first minute is defining. You need to create instant rapport.

Be aware of some simple rules of body language. These poor managers think they understand body language and make false assumptions, so don't give them ammunition to shoot you.

Some tips about body language include;

Don't fidget or look nervous (breathe deeply and stay outwardly calm). This may appear to show dishonesty.

Don't clench your fist or give a sense of aggression.

Do adopt an open posture, relax, face the interviewers, make eye contact and address all of them when answering a question, not just the person who asked it.

Do not look up or to the side when thinking about an answer.

Assumptions may be made unfairly about subconscious motives for the behaviour.

Get the simple things right;

Do completely switch off the phone.

Be polite to everyone including security personnel, receptionists and secretaries.

Find out how people prefer to be addressed (Mr, Mrs, Fred, Frederick . . .) and the correct pronunciation. We live in a cosmopolitan society with people from hundreds of nations living in the area.

Wait to be invited to sit down.

Do not accept a drink unless a glass of water is really necessary. Drinks can only provide a factor which cannot help and can cause mayhem. Imagine the impact of spilling coffee or the clatter of cup and saucer in nervous hands.

Their questions

We cannot predict all of the questions which will be asked. However, some of them are typical or common and you can expect them to occur in many interviews;

<u>Career</u>

Describe the jobs you have done

Describe your last job

What are your achievements?

What have been your successes?

What have been your failures?

What lessons did you learn from each role?

What did you like and dislike about the jobs?

Why did you leave the company or move jobs?

What barriers were there to doing a good job?

Why did you follow this career?

Personal traits

Describe yourself. How would others describe you?

Give three words to describe yourself

What are your strengths? What are your weaknesses?

What motivates you? What demotivates you?

Are you ambitious?

Are you a risk taker? Do you follow rules?

What mechanisms do you use to deal with stress and pressure?

How do you manage projects?

What is your management style?

How do you communicate with your team?

Can you demonstrate you are a team player?

Have you ever been disciplined and, if so, for what?

Rob and Tammy Ball, with Natalie Ball

<u>This application</u>

What have you been doing since your last job?

Why have you applied for this job?

Which other jobs have you applied for?

Have you had any offers?

What do you know about this company? Why are we different?

Can you give examples to provide evidence for your answers?

If we offer you this job will you accept?

Do you have any restrictions to starting work immediately?

Are you willing to travel?

Can we approach your referees?

Who else can we ask about you?

Why have you been unemployed for so long?

Why have you not been successful to date?

The future

Where do you want to be in five or ten years' time?

Do you see yourself in this role for five years?

What are your aims for this job?

How quickly do you want promotion?

What do you see as your major challenges if you are appointed?

Do you like change?

Beyond work

What are your interests?

What are your passions?

How do you balance work and your enthusiasm for other interests?

How do you balance work, interests and home life?

Do you hold any positions of responsibility in any organisation?

Education and training

Why did you choose your degree/diploma/course of study?

Could you have done better in your studies?

Which subjects are most relevant to this application?

Tell me about your on-going training and continuous development

Do you foresee the need for more training for this job?

Will you be able to contribute immediately?

What further education would you like to undertake?

Have you ever thought of completely re-training and changing career?

Do you learn quickly?

What is the purpose of training?

The last few pages have described typical questions. Some interviewers are capable of asking weird ones which, presumably, they feel give an insight of the interviewee;

What did you have for breakfast?

If I gave you a million pounds how would you spend it?

What is your favourite colour, animal, name, film, book . . . ?

When are you happiest?

When are you saddest?

How many people could we get in this room?

Tell me a joke

Do you like my tie?

Be polite but circumspect and if questions are too personal say so.

Answers

Sadly, we cannot give the perfect answer for all questions. However, as your CV will set some of the agenda for an interview you can prepare the outline answer for some of them.

You need to convey the correct impression of competence, ability and enthusiasm. Be wary of the negative questions like, "What are your weaknesses?" Predicting this question may allow an answer like, "I take on too much, so I agree my priorities with my boss and deliver those first", which is much better than, "I can't cope with a heavy workload", an answer which may blurted out by an unprepared person.

Emphasise delivery and achievements.

Give examples to justify your claims. Don't wait to be asked to do so.

Do not tell lies or embellish. Do not use jargon or acronyms.

Do not criticise previous employers, however you may feel.

Do not make statements which will be unsupported by referees or your performance in the job, if you get it.

Ensure your interests support your application. Whilst not making it sound like life is too busy to attend work or you will be a clock watcher, evidence of teamwork, creativity, social conscience and learning will impress.

As you answer questions check with the interviewers you are giving them appropriate answers and not misunderstanding the point. Do not do this every time but show your intelligence and attention to their needs.

Do not just talk. Be as clear and concise as appropriate but ensure the points are covered. If there is a short silence do not feel the urge to fill it with irrelevances and damaging information you didn't intend to reveal.

Let the interviewers talk. They will help you by providing guidance in the way the company operates and their thinking. If there is a long diatribe followed by, "Do you agree?" say so, unless you really disagree and don't add too much. However, if this is a subject about which you have a lot of examples, it is a great opportunity.

Be wary of provocation. If the interview is designed to be highly pressured you must maintain your poise and objectivity.

Do not let the interview close with vital points unmade. Normally, there is a final question like, "Do you want to tell us anything else?" Have a mental checklist and if there are areas to be covered do so now. It may feel like the interviewers want to conclude the conversation, so add a statement such as, "I have a very relevant point . . ." Do not leave the room wishing you had remembered to say things or had been bold enough to take the time to make them.

In your answers try to convey;

Your principles. Think about how you want to be perceived and how to achieve it.

Your skills. More than a list of qualifications and training courses.

Your personality. What makes you tick, why you can work with people and how success is primarily about the business and personal pride comes second.

Your ambition for the business but how you can develop at the same time. Progression for yourself will be achieved through delivery.

Personal honesty. If you are true to yourself they can trust you to be honest with them.

What makes your heart soar? Enthusiasm is natural and not many people can fake it. Let them know what matters to you.

Your questions

As we stated earlier this is both a chance to learn more to make a decision if the job is offered and to make a positive impression;

Do ask about the organisation, its direction and ambitions.

Do not ask about pay rises or likely promotions.

Demonstrate your interest in them.

Do not come across as being clever just for the sake of it.

Do sound professional and genuine.

Do not appear to be slick and pompous.

Do show a level of understanding about the company.

Do not allow the inference you are asking questions to which you already know the answer.

Even though you have prepared questions be careful not to ask something which has been discussed. Therefore, have a number of questions to ask and do it throughout the interview, in a natural way, not just at the end in a stage managed manner.

You may ask about the next stages of the process. Indicate your enthusiasm for the role. If it is clear that this is the final stage it is appropriate to ask about pay and benefits. Do not be surprised if there is a fixed rate-of-pay or any negotiations are to take place in the event of a job offer. If you were put forward by a professional agency it may take the role of negotiator. Clarify this at the outset with the agency.

You may be asked about salary aspirations. In preparation you must have considered this. Clues could come from a number of sources—there may be an indication in the advertisement, you have a minimum acceptable level anyway, similar roles may have been in the paper, the agency may have given you an indication and your market research will help.

Whilst you don't want to say a figure which is too low, there is also a concern a candidate of similar quality will ask for less and, therefore get the job. What feels fair? Do they have a figure in mind? How many options do you have? If in doubt and pressed for an answer, give a number but also ask about other benefits which may influence the salary you are prepared to accept. This puts it back to the company to make a proposal.

It is fair to ask about timescales. Good practice may well have ensured this is clear but it is not impolite to ask if it hasn't.

Conclude very politely, even if it has been a grilling. Thank the interviewers and confirm your continued interest in the job.

Personal style

Nobody attends an interview wanting to make a bad impression. However, too often people pitch it wrongly. Some are arrogant and talkative, others are shy and mute. Each person needs to decide their own approach. Certainly, the assessors must hear the evidence to support the application. Even the best interviewers cannot recognise your genius if you hide it from them.

We describe the Confidence Continuum, on which 0 is total silence and no contribution to the discussion and 10 is unswervingly boastful behaviour.

The balance is confident and humble; open and respectful; participative and attentive.

Perhaps the score, on this notional scale should be about 7 or 8. This is no more than a guide to help people think about style.

Post interview actions

As there may be another interview, even if it was indicated there wouldn't be, make notes for yourself;

Who were the interviewers?

What were they actually interested in?

Which elements of the CV were covered most thoroughly?

What did they emphasise?

Which points do you need to research further?

What lessons must you learn for interviews with this company or more generally?

Feedback to the recruitment consultant if there is one. Keep the people on your side included.

If you are recalled, do all of the preparation again but assisted by the experience of the previous meeting. Take nothing for granted.

Notes

Chapter 8

Pre-judgements regarding age

Life isn't just for people in their thirties

Older candidates

What are the concerns?

Now we deal in stereotypes, generalisations and myths;

- Absence is higher amongst older people. WRONG, it is seen to be about the same
- People slow down as they get older. Partially TRUE, so don't put them in production work in a physically demanding environment but use their skills appropriately
- Older folk are less flexible. WRONG, some are less flexible as are some youngsters. It is a state of mind not body. When introducing a new organisation some years ago we did some research in the workforce and the over 50's were markedly more positive about change than any other group. They had the experience to deal with it and not be frightened by the unknown

- Speed of thought is slower. WRONG, and the individuals have a much wider span of knowledge
- If an employee is older the time in job will be less. WRONG, in many cases. As a counter point, graduates typically spend less than 3 years with their first employer. Recruit a 55 year old and realistically expect 10 years' service
- Older people are technophobic. WRONG, no more than some younger folk. Anyone not trained will be incapable of using any piece of kit, regardless of levels of complexity
- Training is a waste of time and money. WRONG, no more so than for anyone else and these are potential employees who will stay longer, as shown above
- Young people are more effective. WRONG, studies show there is little difference
- Employees go on past 65, clog up promotional opportunities and really slow down. WRONG, some 65 year olds are invaluable and it is imperative they are retained

What have older people got to offer?

Aside from specific role-related skills, they may have;

- Years of applying their skills and knowledge
- A work ethic
- Actually achieved things, they are not just potential for the future, they are the here for now and tomorrow
- Better relationship building approaches
- Loyalty, and even more so if a company gives them a chance
- Motivation stimulated by the opportunity
- Abilities to mentor, coach and guide
- Freedom from children complications
- Flexibility to work different shift patterns or hours
- Less burning ambition for the next job and more ambition to do this job well and a love of being at work
- A willingness to learn new skills and apply them rather than to put them on the CV for the benefit of another employer
- An ability to relate to the particular clientele of a business

Actions for the older person

Actions anyone can take come under four headings;

- Research
- Consideration
- Preparation
- Negotiation

1) Research
   - Google "Older Workers" to find specific organisations to help
   - Find companies with good policies e.g. B+Q, Cadbury Schweppes, BBC, BT, Wetherspoons
   - Research companies' principles and policies

2)   Consideration

- Salary and contract
- Relocation
- Status/prestige
- Pension
- Shifts/hours
- Permanent/Interim/Temporary
- Type of employment e.g. retail, customer service, call centres, sales, manufacturing

The next two headings are where real support for older unemployed people can be developed. Very often candidates for vacancies are of a similar strength, so a small percentage improvement may make the difference between success and failure to get the job.

3)   Preparation

-    Address honestly the issue of State of Mind. If there is a concern it may be unemployment itself that is causing it, the length of time unemployed, the reasons for losing the previous job (which might be age) or the perceived reasons for not being able to find another position
-    Learn all of the messages in the rest of this book about the CV, interview and taking personal control
-    Construct answers. Not just to the obvious questions that will be posed but also have answers to use to convey the correct messages (committed, loyal, intelligent, mentally agile, fit, mature in the correct sense of the word, change agent, masses of common sense, great balance of energy and vast experience, not scared of change and principled)

- Plan how you will break the stereotype
- Volunteer. Better to be seen to be positive and to operate in different working environments
- Learn new skills, and not just the basics
- Take a temporary job
- Have physically demanding hobbies
- Have stimulating hobbies
- Have a medical, prove you are fit and healthy (or if not describe limits and how well you can work within them)
- Take psychometric tests to practice and feel comfortable with them

4)   Negotiation

It is still about giving messages but without looking desperate. What are the variables which can be addressed?

-   Options

        Flexible contract
        Unpopular hours to start
        Salary
        Pension
        Alternative benefits

-   Start Date—presumably immediate
-   Flexibility
-   Not looking for promotion and, therefore, not a
    threat to the interviewer

Younger candidates

All of the principles of job hunt apply but which messages can inexperienced people emphasise?

- Enthusiasm
- Energy
- Potential for the future
- Recently in education
- Thirsting for knowledge and skills
- No pre-judgements
- Flexible and unconstrained
- Ambitious

The key is preparation and a conviction about the advantages of employing YOU. How can the advantages best be communicated?

Construct answers. As with older people, not just to the obvious questions that will be posed but also have answers to use to convey the correct messages (committed, loyal, intelligent, mentally adroit, fit, mature beyond years, adaptable, common sense already, great balance of energy and enthusiasm, accepts change and has a base of principles and ethics).

What evidence is there to support these claims? Remember participation in extra-curricular activities whilst in education, voluntary work, positions of responsibility in sports clubs, membership of organisations and events organisation can allow many transferrable skills and traits to be displayed.

Notes

Chapter 9

Dealing with rejection

Finding positive aspects from not getting a job

It is a statistical fact that for most people it is inevitable any specific application will not be successful. If twenty people apply for one job, nineteen are going to meet rejection at some point in the process.

But is it rejection or failure?

These are highly emotive and pejorative terms. It is not a personal rejection, albeit it affects you (and your family) personally. Businesses do not make recruitment decisions on subjective criteria. The task is to find the most appropriate person for the role; the candidate whose skills and traits are best aligned. If that isn't you, you will not get the job. Not because you are a "bad person" or useless but because there was a better fit applicant. You didn't fail to get the job but someone else succeeded.

It is, therefore, really important that you and people around you stop using rejection and failure as terms. Harmlessly meant but with potentially profound effects.

Your expectations will be a self-fulfilling prophecy. If you do not expect to acquire a particular position it is certain you won't. It is tricky enough to get a job without you making the decision on behalf of the recruiter. Allow negative thoughts into the psyche and there will only be negative outcomes. So, even though the words are not designed to hurt, rejection and failure will rapidly undermine the confidence of the job hunter.

Be rational and think about the process—numerous candidates with a wide range of experience means just getting an interview is a success.

The psychology of applying

Merely applying for a job takes some courage. You are asking to be judged and no-one likes any inference of criticism, yet that is the essence of the whole process. Recognise this at the outset and mentally prepare for the consequences.

Words and platitudes are easy and a stream of applications not achieving the desired result will be exhausting emotionally. Are you ready to acknowledge one possible road has closed (but only one of many)? Are your family attuned to these likely results?

Actors live their lives like this. Now, they have consciously chosen a profession fraught with obstacles;

Few jobs

Very many highly talented competitors

The need to perform wonderfully in a range of situations

The whims of directors and producers

Actors deal with a wide spectrum of variables, some of which are personal;

Too tall, too short

Wrong accent

Not attractive enough, wrong sort of good looks

Hair colour not quite as visualised

Look older/younger than their photograph

Too nervous, too confident

How can they cope with the frustrations of preparation, performance and being unsuccessful in 99% of the auditions? It is all about State of Mind and acceptance. Having been to an audition the only thing to do is forget it and prepare for the next one. Actors typically are not even given the courtesy of a "Dear John". Usually, only the successful person hears the result. It is the same mindset for all job applications.

We mentioned earlier there are some organisations from which there will be little communication, not even an acknowledgement despite the fact the correspondence has been electronic.

This may be caused by the volume of people expressing an interest, simply poor processes or the desire to save money. It is very poor behaviour and unacceptable. If it doesn't go well you may console yourself that working for such a company would have been difficult anyway.

Some employment agencies are as bad, even if they contact you. We touched on this earlier. It may be better to set expectation levels quite low and then be delighted by the professional ones.

Infrequently, timescales are given, although in some public sectors it seems deadlines are more important than finding the correct person. Go with the flow and don't let the foibles of others be too influential on your professionalism.

Areas for improvement

In moving on to the next job application, it is crucial there is an honest critique of the last one.

If the vacancies seem relevant and interviews are not forthcoming it is important the CV and the accompanying letters are reviewed. Are they really meeting the needs of the recruiter? Do they do you justice? Do you impress you and your family in these documents?

Do re-read the application forms. Did you say what you really wanted to and clearly enough? Are the critical words and phrases there? Are you certain the application arrived? Did you receive an acknowledgement? Did you include a stamped addressed envelope (sae) if it was required? Was there a deadline date and was it met?

If there was an interview how can the performance be improved?

Were nerves overpowering? Were you confident you knew for which job you were being interviewed? Had you read the CV again and again? Had you rehearsed the messages which were critical to creating the best impression?

Were you there on time? What was the first impression you made? How was your appearance? Were there difficult questions? Did the interviewers ask about areas of your background you didn't expect? Which answers seemed to make the best impact?

Did you ask questions?

What feedback have you received?

Some of these answers may be uncomfortable but personal honesty has rarely been more important.

Even small improvements will make a difference, including to your confidence. Was there a little issue such as thinking you wished you had brought a clean handkerchief? It may seem trivial but distracting and easily put right next time.

Did you do EVERYTHING you could have or was there some compromise or inattention to detail? "It will do" is absolutely not an acceptable standard.

Proper preparation prevents poor performance.

It is in your compass and control, don't concede it. You know what to do, so do it.

Notes

Chapter 10

Dealing with offers

Success but with eyes wide open

Considerations

In theory, in the abstract world of advisors, we would recommend that anyone takes adequate time to make a mature and rational decision regarding a job offer. However, context is everything. If the mortgage needs to be paid, bills are mounting and the cupboard is bare there may be an exceedingly pressing reason to accept any offer and move on.

Remember you will receive at least one job offer. However, there is the Law of Buses; you wait for a long time for one, then two or more come at the same time. If they are simultaneous the decision will be straightforward because you have already thought through the preferred criteria and pursued those jobs. You can assess the variables and accept the job which suits best.

More problematic is the sense a better job offer may be coming, so is it right to wait and hope or accept the bird in the hand?

Can there be negotiations? Is the salary adequate? Is there relocation? Bonus? Upon what criteria is bonus paid?

What are the personal implications of location, hours, overtime, travel, staying away from home or the status of the role? If the last position was in management and this is solely as a team member will it be easy to adapt?

Will there be a need for re-training? Who pays for training and where will it be?

Is this company in trouble or has the research shown it is stable or growing?

How long is the probation period and what are the criteria upon which the decision be taken at the end of it?

Are there actually "red hot" leads for more attractive positions?

Think carefully but be wary of finding excuses not to decide. It is easy to find the current lack of responsibilities attractive and justify to yourself not working.

Occasionally, a job offer is made at the end of an interview. Having been very enthusiastic about the job for an hour or so, there may be some doubt or the prospect of another offer. Thank the interviewer, indicate your desire to take the job, give a timescale for final answer and make a polite excuse such as discussing it with your partner, as you do with all major decisions.

It is a great position to be in but do not abuse it by over delaying your decision. An offer can be withdrawn.

References

References are not always taken up but typically they are. Therefore,

- Ensure contact details are correct for quoted referees
- Confirm the people are willing to be a referee
- Recognise the company may do other checks
- Previous employers will probably be contacted
- Self-employed people's clients may be questioned
- Qualifications may be checked. Have certificates available
- Social media may be reviewed. If there would be any embarrassment from a post do not write it. Do keep all detail up-to-date if it will help applications

We live in an electronic age and it becomes more difficult to maintain secrets.

Probation period

Usually, companies will expect new hires to complete a three to six month probation. The law is such that if anyone is unsatisfactory it is simple to dismiss them. The organisation should still follow proper process for fairness, to give the new person time to correct any shortcomings and to eliminate any accusation of discrimination.

The use of a probation period recognises people take time to settle, learn the procedures, meet people and pick up the role. These may be overlaid with significant training. So, understand against which criteria assessment will be made.

Do be enthusiastic, integrate, learn, improve and contribute (even if some misgivings remain). Show progressively targets will be met.

Do not express any concerns regarding the decision to join the new employer.

What if the new job is not right?

Our first recommendation is spend at least a year in a role before making moves to leave; see the whole cycle. Joining accounts at the end of the financial year will not be a good time to base a judgement about workload, so hold tight and experience it all.

Is the job as it was described?

Have your aspirations changed?

What is wrong or is it a reaction to the initial excitement of getting the job?

Can things be altered?

What is difficult/boring/challenging?

Who can help?

What does the family think?

Leaving the new job

Employers will be seriously annoyed if you accept a job with them and then, subsequently, leave to take another position for which you were under consideration when you accepted their offer. It is probable good people were rejected; it is certain there are costs associated with finding someone else.

A contract of employment was entered in good faith. It is a legal contract and applies equally to organisations and individuals.

Personal reputation will be harmed. Nobody should seek to be thought of as untrustworthy or frivolous.

Is job-hopping really a symptom of a quest to find a company like the one from which you were dismissed? If so, accept it cannot be replicated and realise this is an excellent alternative. Different is good, not bad.

Notes

Chapter 11

Alternatives to a job

Wage slave or finding other routes to satisfaction

Possibilities

There are countless alternatives to traditional employment but to consider a few;

- Self employment
- Franchise purchase
- Retirement
- Semi-retirement
- Housewife/husband/partner

In all cases seek advice and guidance. Find experts who can give facts but also ask excellent questions. Taking one of these options is not necessarily forever but they are big steps.

Self-employment

Hopefully, this won't just be a reaction to the frustrations of job hunting. It shouldn't be a case of, "I can't find a job, so I will work for myself".

There must be a desire to be self-employed. It is different, has many additional pressures and requires many extra skills.

There must be an idea and, preferably, a passion.

Funding is always a big issue. What are the real start-up costs and for how long can the business operate before there must be a healthy profit?

What structure should it be? Is there a business partner? Ought it to be a limited company or a partnership? Who owns the business? How are decisions made?

How will work be found?

How to market the business?

Are experts needed for advice?

Is a lawyer or accountant needed?

Which insurances are required?

How is a bank account set up?

Who can sign cheques?

How is advertising organised?

What happens in the case of illness?

What will the effect be on holidays?

What are the implications associated with employing people?

Are benefits still payable?

These questions merely scratch the surface of the challenges to be addressed.

Franchise purchase

One method of acquiring a product for self-employment is to purchase a franchise. Thousands exist covering a wide range of subjects, such as travel, car repair, shop signs and fast food outlets.

There will be an initial payment plus a monthly charge or a percentage cut or both. This may well be fair if the franchisor takes on a lot of the administration. Be clear the product is good, find out what is included in the package and carry out research. Talk to other franchisees with the company. Ask how many hours are involved, if the bureaucracy is easy, how much is spent on advertising, what is the turnover of franchisees and if there is a strong reputation?

Take advice from professionals and ensure there are no surprises.

Retirement

It may be possible. Having reviewed all of the financial aspects it may be the best option. Life may be a little different but more relaxed and pleasurable.

If there is a wife/husband/partner still working it may be a great idea and a chance to do more fulfilling things.

Or it may be semi-retirement; a part-time job in something different—classroom assistant or technician, careers advisor, gardener, charity worker . . .

Housewife/husband/partner

If there are children it could be it is better for the currently unemployed partner to stay at home; save on the cost of a child minder, be confident the youngsters are being brought up well and supplement income by working from home.

Do not allow the thinking to be constrained by what has been or the subjective views of other people.

It is very worthwhile investigating the options of homeworking. As ever, the internet is a potential gold mine but with the caveat that the unscrupulous lie in wait for the unsuspecting.

Notes

Conclusion

- The job now is to ensure employment or decide upon an alternative. Keeping the current one may well be a better prospect than seeking an alternative immediately. It is certainly true it is easier to find another job when in employment. Avoid the wisdom of hindsight—if only I hadn't taken so much time off or been late frequently; I wish I had paid more attention to the projects I was given and realised quality mattered. Your work is your responsibility not your manager's.

- Finding a job is a difficult process for the candidate AND for the recruiter. Too many managers prefer to avoid people issues. This gives you the chance to make an impression by making it easy for the recruiter to like you, appreciate your capabilities and hire you. Seek the little things which can make a difference.

- Emotions must be channelled and attitudes must be positive. Do not ever criticise a previous employer. It cannot help the application.

- Control the controllables and don't worry about the things over which you have no influence. If a vacancy for which you had a great deal of optimism is cancelled, move on. It has gone and it wasn't your fault. It may be frustrating but energies need to be focused on the other positions available.

- Similarly, it is better not to build up your own hopes too high, or those of loved ones. Deal in facts not conjecture; manage expectations.

- Think deeply about what you really want, why you are in this position, who can help, which companies or industries are interesting and how to be successful. Five minutes of proper thought is worth several hours of unfocused effort.

- Be diligent, take care to be accurate, research thoroughly and approach the exercise professionally. To do these well and to make the process easy it will be necessary to have access to the internet.

- People matter if this is to be successful. Networking is crucial but do not see it as just other people giving to you. Support friends and ex-colleagues in the same position. It is a truism the more you give, the more you receive.

- Listen and do not stop thinking and looking. It is impossible to predict when and from where the opportunity will occur.

- There are mountains of advice out there but be wary of template CV's and letters. Imprint yourself on correspondence and display your many positive attributes which are available to a prospective employer.

- Recognise there will be times when you feel there is unfairness in the outcomes. If there has been illegal behaviour deal with it but often it is a sense you were a perfectly good candidate but failed to secure the job. It happens and there are others for which to apply. Move on.

- Keep reviewing your performance for ways to do better. Little things do matter.

- Your time should be dedicated to acquiring a job, to the relevant processes and making sure your application is as good as it possibly can be.

- Look after yourself both physically and mentally. Use this time well to develop and grow.

- Keep up personal morale. Seek assistance when it becomes difficult.

Proper preparation prevents poor performance

So, you know what to do

Do you actually prepare or do you still expect to be able to busk and blag it? Too many people, even after reading this book and talking to friends, will go to an interview expecting to impress without any preparation or rehearsal.

Is it easier to assume high level performance without expending any energy to achieve it? For some people there is a natural confidence or arrogance which prevents them from making any effort. It won't always be alright on the night. The messages from every profession show success comes from thought, practice and preparation.

Is it a good excuse for dealing with a lack of success? For a few people failure to be ready for the process is a defence mechanism, "It is everyone else's fault, not mine!"

Nothing described in this book is beyond anyone. Whether it is attempting to maintain the current role, deciding what is next or the job hunt process; they can be addressed methodically and rigorously.

The biggest complications are the scale of competition and the scope for personal performance to vary. So, each candidate is seeking their edge, the extra advantage over other people. If you can make ten improvements which give just 0.5% better opportunity each, that is 5% improvement; a phenomenal boost. Of course, it is possible everyone else is getting this 5% but what chance have you got if you are not acting equally as professionally?

The final aspect is luck, such as ringing someone just as a vacancy becomes available or supporting the same team as the interviewer. However, we can, to a large degree, make our own luck through preparation and application.

We hope you have a great deal of success.

We would love to discuss these ideas and any others which matter to you.

In the first instance contact us through;

rob.ball@naturallyconcerned.com

or visit

www.naturallyconcerned.com

Authors

Rob Ball   BSc., Chartered FCIPD, MIoD, MIACE

Rob is British and a founder and director of Naturally Concerned (for Alison) Ltd. Naturally Concerned is committed to leadership development, personal advocacy, travel, animal conservation, improving the environment and stimulating people to think about the critical issues facing us.

Rob is a career, life and business coach.

Formerly, he was in Human Resources for 30 years, working for MG Rover Group and GKN in senior roles. He continues to act as a HR advisor to different organisations.

Tammy Ball   BA, MLS

Tammy is from Oklahoma City in the United States of America. She has a Master of Liberal Studies degree from the University of Oklahoma and a Bachelor of Business Administration from the University of Central Oklahoma. Tammy has been employed by the state of Oklahoma for more than 10 years. She specialises in Change Leadership.

Tammy is a career, life and business coach.

Natalie Ball   BA

Natalie, daughter of Rob, also a founder and director of Naturally Concerned (for Alison) Ltd.

Natalie is a professional actor and graduate of Bristol Old Vic Theatre School.

www.naturallyconcerned.com